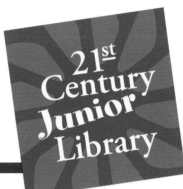

URANUS

by Ariel Kazunas

CHERRY LAKE PUBLISHING * ANN ARBOR, MICHIGAN

Published in the United States of America by Cherry Lake Publishing
Ann Arbor, Michigan
www.cherrylakepublishing.com

Content Adviser: Dr. Tobias Owen, University of Hawaii Institute for Astronomy

Photo Credits: Cover, ©Orlando Florin Rosu/Dreamstime.com; cover and page 6, ©Kevin Schley/Alamy; cover and page 8, ©MichaelTaylor/Shutterstock, Inc.; cover and pages 10 and 18, ©NASA; page 4, ©Orla/Shutterstock, Inc.; page 12, ©iStockphoto.com/larslentz; page 14, ©maryo/Shutterstock, Inc.; page 16, ©Sabino Parente/Shutterstock, Inc.; page 20, ©Mark Garlick/Alamy

LIBRARY OF CONGRESS CATALOGING-IN-PUBLICATION DATA

Kazunas, Ariel.
  Uranus/by Ariel Kazunas.
    p. cm.—(21st century junior library)
  Includes bibliographical references and index.
  ISBN-13: 978-1-61080-084-6 (lib. bdg.)
  ISBN-10: 1-61080-084-2 (lib. bdg.)
  1. Uranus (Planet)—Juvenile literature. I. Title.
QB681.K39 2011
523.47—dc22   2010052610

Cherry Lake Publishing would like to acknowledge the work of
The Partnership for 21st Century Skills.
Please visit www.21stcenturyskills.org for more information.

Printed in the United States of America
Corporate Graphics Inc.
July 2011
CLFA09

CONTENTS

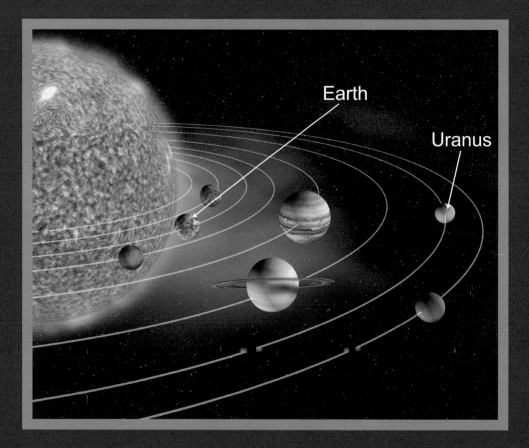

Earth

Uranus

Uranus is very far from both Earth and the Sun.

Comet or Planet?

Our **solar system** has eight planets. They all travel around the Sun. Uranus is the seventh planet from the Sun.

Uranus is more than 1.7 billion miles (2.7 billion kilometers) from Earth. This makes it very hard to see in the night sky.

A comet streaks through the sky. William Herschel thought he was looking at a comet when he first saw Uranus.

Uranus was not discovered until 1781. An **astronomer** named William Herschel saw it through a **telescope**.

Uranus looked like a **comet** through Herschel's telescope. **Scientists** later figured out that it was a planet.

Look!

Try looking for Uranus in the night sky. It is easiest to find when you are far away from any lights. A telescope will also help. Your teacher or librarian can help you find out where to look.

Uranus' blue color comes from the gases that make up most of the planet.

What Is It Like on Uranus?

Uranus does not have a solid surface as Earth does. It is a big blue ball of gas. The planet's core is probably made of rock and ice. But scientists are not sure yet.

TITAN/CENTAUR COMPLEX 41

The *Voyager 2* spacecraft helped scientists learn more about Uranus and other faraway planets.

Uranus travels around the Sun. The path it takes is called its **orbit**. The time it takes to go around the Sun one time is called a year.

Uranus has a long orbit. This is because it is so far from the Sun. Its years are very long. One year on Uranus is as long as 84 Earth years!

Ask Questions!

A NASA spacecraft called *Voyager 2* collected information about Uranus. How do you think *Voyager 2* collected this information? Ask a teacher or librarian to help you learn more about *Voyager 2* and NASA.

The outer parts of Uranus are very cold.

Temperatures at the top of Uranus's clouds are very cold. They can get as low as −366 degrees Fahrenheit (−221 degrees Celsius).

Scientists think the inside of Uranus is much hotter. The middle of the planet might be as hot as 12,600°F (6,982°C)!

Most planets in our solar system have an axis that points up and down like Earth's does.

Spinning Sideways

Uranus **rotates** differently than other planets. Every other planet in our solar system spins with its **axis** pointing up and down. But Uranus looks as if it has been knocked on its side. It spins with its axis pointing from side to side.

No other planet in our solar system has an axis like Uranus's.

Scientists think Uranus used to spin like the other planets. A very big object probably rammed into Uranus. This tipped the planet on its side.

Create!

Try sticking a pencil through the middle of a foam ball. Hold the pencil straight up and spin it. This is how most planets rotate. Now turn the pencil on its side and spin it. This is how Uranus rotates!

Miranda is the fifth-largest of Uranus's moons.

Rings, Moons, and More

There are 27 known moons orbiting Uranus. Most of them are very small.

Uranus also has at least 10 rings. The rings were discovered in 1977.

Make a Guess!

Uranus's rings curve around the planet in a different direction than the ones around other planets. Why do you think this is? Could it have something to do with the way Uranus rotates?

What secrets does Uranus hold?

There is a lot left to learn about Uranus. New tools will help scientists gather more information about this faraway planet. What will we find out next?

Create! Try drawing a picture of Uranus. Find a shade of blue that is just right. Look at a picture to make sure you put the rings in the right place.

GLOSSARY

astronomer (uh-STRON-uh-mur) someone who studies stars, planets, and space

axis (AK-siss) an imaginary line that goes through an object and around which the object turns

comet (KOM-it) a piece of rock or ice that orbits the Sun

orbit (OR-bit) to travel in a path around a central point

rotates (ROH-tayts) spins

scientists (SYE-uhn-tists) people who study nature and make discoveries

solar system (SOH-lur SISS-tuhm) a star, such as the Sun, and all the planets and moons that move around it

telescope (TEL-uh-skohp) a tool used to look at faraway objects

FIND OUT MORE

BOOKS

Aguilar, David A. *11 Planets: A New View of the Solar System.* Washington, DC: National Geographic Society, 2008.

Landau, Elaine. *Uranus.* New York: Children's Press, 2008.

Vogt, Gregory. *Uranus.* Minneapolis: Lerner Publications, 2010.

WEB SITES

HubbleSite Gallery
hubblesite.org/gallery
Take a look at some cool pictures of outer space.

NASA: Solar System Exploration
solarsystem.nasa.gov/kids
Check out these fun activities from NASA.

Space.com—Our Solar System: Facts, Formation and Discovery
www.space.com/solarsystem/
Learn more about the objects in our solar system and how they were formed.

INDEX

ABOUT THE AUTHOR

Ariel Kazunas lives on the Oregon coast, writing books for kids and working at the Sitka Center for Art and Ecology. She has also worked for several nonprofit magazines. Ariel loves exploring our planet, Earth—especially by hand, foot, bike, and boat—and camping out under the stars.